In this book, we're going to talk about the timeline of the Civil War. So, let's get right to it!

WHAT WAS THE CIVIL WAR?

The Civil War in the United States and the events that led up to the start of it lasted from 1860 through 1865. One of the major issues that split the states was the issue of slavery. People in the North felt that slavery was ethically wrong and they wanted to end it. People who felt strongly that slaves should be set free were called abolitionists.

THE AMERICAN CIVIL WAR
BLUES, GREYS, YANKEES AND REBELS

HISTORY FOR KIDS

HISTORICAL TIMELINES FOR KIDS

5TH GRADE SOCIAL STUDIES

The southern states depended on slave labor for their farms and plantations. They were concerned that they wouldn't be able to keep their businesses profitable without the labor of slaves. The southern states didn't want the northern states to dictate the laws so they seceded from the Union, which simply meant they didn't want to be part of the United States anymore. They wanted to be their own country, the Confederacy. The northern states wanted the United States to remain as one country, so the Civil War broke out.

WHO WERE THE YANKEES AND THE REBELS?

The Yankees were the soldiers who were fighting for the North and the Rebels were the soldiers who were fighting for the South. When the Civil War started, neither side expected a long and drawn-out war. Neither side had proper uniforms for their men.

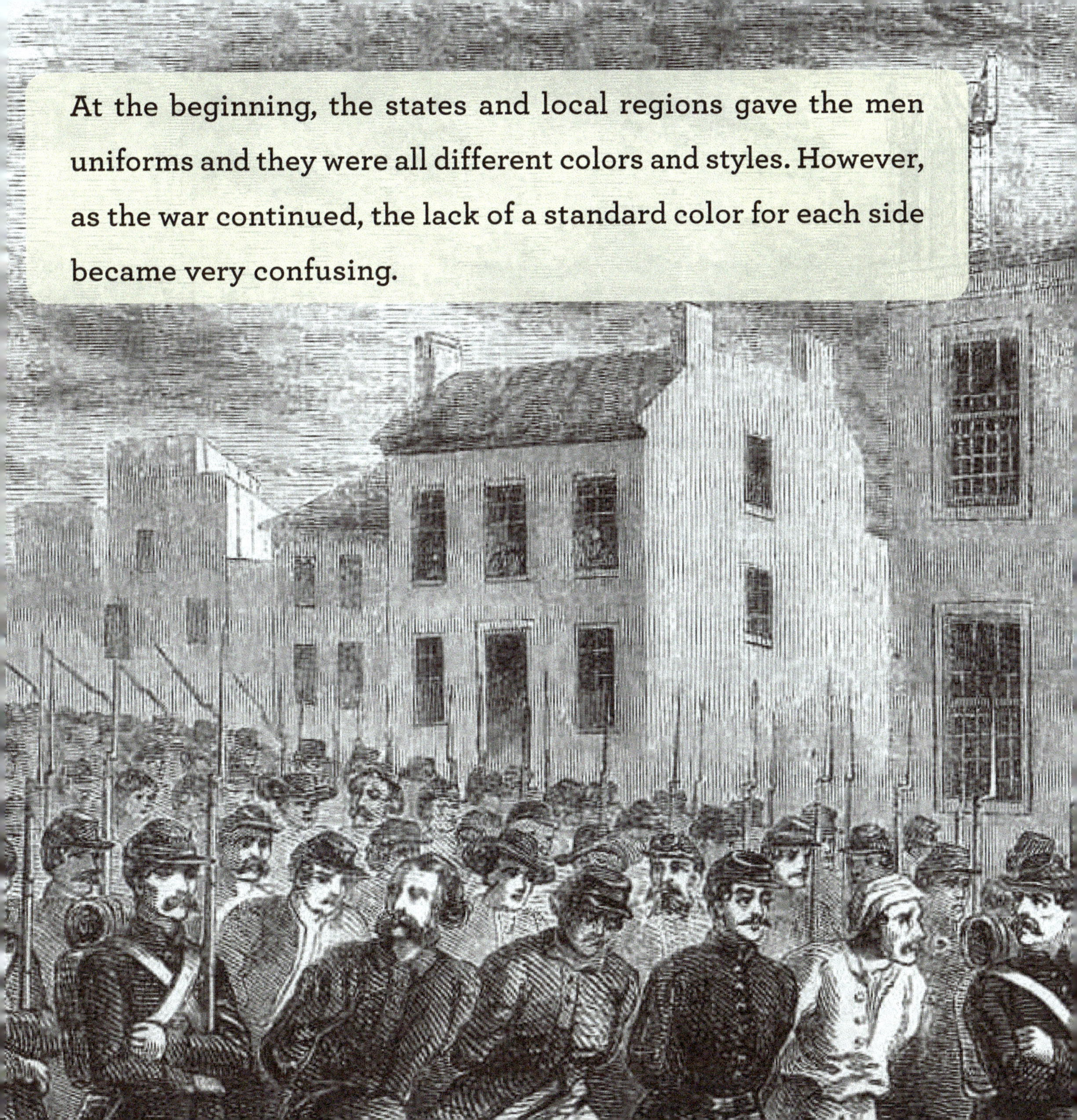
At the beginning, the states and local regions gave the men uniforms and they were all different colors and styles. However, as the war continued, the lack of a standard color for each side became very confusing.

At times there were deadly consequences as men shot soldiers who were on their side instead of on the enemy's side. Eventually, the Union or North had dark blue for their standard uniforms and the Confederacy or South had grey for theirs.

TIMELINE OF THE CIVIL WAR

The following timeline lists some of the major events in the war between the Yankees and the Rebels.

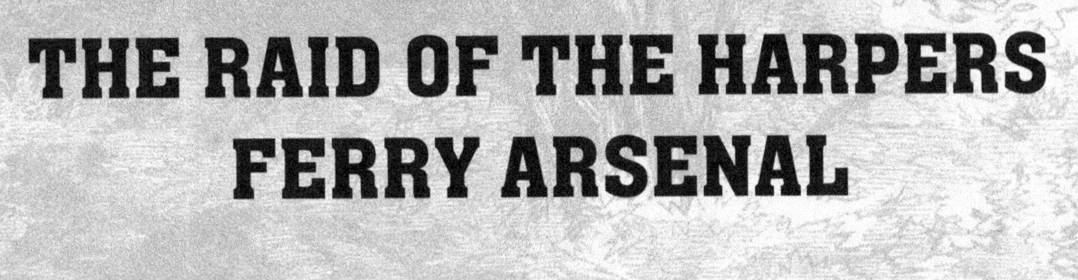

THE RAID OF THE HARPERS FERRY ARSENAL

John Brown was a white man who felt that slavery was wrong. He was upset that other abolitionists weren't using forceful means to put an end to slavery. He began a plan to arm the slaves so they could rise up and fight against their masters.

There was a well-stocked arsenal at Harpers Ferry in Virginia and it was his plan to take over the arsenal and give the weapons to the slaves so they could fight. On October 16 in the year 1859, he tried to get control of the arsenal, but he wasn't successful. He was captured and then hanged for his crime. However, many people in the northern states thought he was a hero. Less than a year after the Harpers Ferry raid, the war broke out.

W.G.STEPHENS

ABRAHAM LINCOLN

THE PRESIDENTIAL ELECTION

Abraham Lincoln was elected as President of the United States on November 6 in the year 1860. The northern states wanted him in office. One of the reasons was he agreed with the abolitionists that slavery should end. Before Lincoln had his official inauguration in January of 1861, some southern states began to leave the Union because they didn't want to lose their slaves.

SOUTH CAROLINA LEAVES THE UNION

On the 20th of December in 1860, the state of South Carolina officially left the Union. South Carolina was the first to secede but soon many other states followed.

Mississippi and Florida seceded on January 9 and 10

Alabama followed on January 11

Georgia seceded on January 19

Louisiana followed on January 26

Texas seceded on February 1

SOUTH CAROLINA

JEFFERSON DAVIS

THE CONFEDERACY WAS ESTABLISHED

On the 9th of February in 1861, before Lincoln began his presidency, the Confederacy was established. The southern states that had seceded now considered themselves to be a separate country, the Confederate States of America. They elected their own president, Jefferson Davis.

Slavery wasn't the only issue in the secession of the southern states. The southern states were opposed to a strong national government. They preferred for states to be in charge of their own laws. More western states were joining the United States and the southern states felt that they would lose their power.

ALABAMA STATE CAPITOL BUILDING

The Confederate States of America became its own government. They issued money and had their own capital city. They also tried to form alliances with other countries such as Great Britain to help them fight, but they weren't successful in doing this, which ultimately hurt them.

ABRAHAM LINCOLN BECAME PRESIDENT

As of March the 4th in the year 1861, Lincoln was President of the United States and was ready to move forward to unite the country once again. Lincoln was shocked that the southern states had decided to secede. He didn't think the tensions would erupt into war.

THE CIVIL WAR

THE WAR BEGINS AT FORT SUMTER

On the 12th of April in 1861, tensions between Union and Confederate forces erupted when Rebel soldiers attacked the Union army at Fort Sumter in the Confederate state of South Carolina. The Civil War had begun.

THE FORT SUMTER

US CONFEDERATE NATIONAL FLAG

MORE STATES SECEDED

Now that the war had begun in earnest, four more states, Virginia, Tennessee, North Carolina, and Arkansas all seceded to join the Confederate states in April of 1861.

A UNION BLOCKADE WAS ANNOUNCED

Hoping to shorten any violence, Lincoln announced on the 19th of April 1861 that the Union navy would prohibit supplies from going into or out of the Confederate states. This blockade became more effective as the war dragged on.

THE BATTLES BETWEEN 1861 AND 1862

The battles between the North and South reached a peak during this year. Many soldiers were wounded and many never came back to their families.

Some of the major battles were:

- The First Battle of Bull Run, a Confederate victory
- The Battle of Shiloh, a Union victory
- The inconclusive sea battle of the ships called the Monitor and the Merrimac, which had iron plates on their sides

THE EMANCIPATION PROCLAMATION

On the 1st of January in 1863, Lincoln issued the Emancipation Proclamation. It stated that all slaves in the Rebel states would be set free. In other words, it had an immediate effect for slaves that lived in the Confederate States not under the control of the North. This proclamation made it possible for black slaves to become free men and join the Union army to fight for freedom. The Emancipation Proclamation paved the way for the 13th Amendment to the Constitution that would outlaw slavery.

THE BATTLE OF GETTYSBURG

The Battle of Gettysburg occurred on the 1st of July in 1863. It was a major battle and it represented a turning point in the war due to the decisive victory of the Union troops. It was the deadliest of the war's battles with almost 8,000 fatalities. Later that year in the month of November, Lincoln gave a speech at the cemetery in Gettysburg, Pennsylvania. The speech wasn't long, but it turned out to be one of the greatest speeches in history.

SHERMAN CAPTURED ATLANTA

General Sherman, who was commanding the Union forces, captured Atlanta in the state of Georgia on the 2nd of September in the year 1864. Later that same year, he and his troops destroyed industries and farms as they burned the land on their path from Atlanta to Savannah. He divided his troops into four different groups so that the Confederate troops weren't sure what his final destination was.

WILLIAM T. SHERMAN

It's estimated that Sherman and his army destroyed $100 million in property based on the value of United States dollars in 1864. This decisive victory for the Union was called "Sherman's March to the Sea."

ROBERT E. LEE SURRENDERS

General Robert E. Lee, the head of the army of the Confederate states, surrendered to the Union commander, General Ulysses S. Grant. This event was the beginning of the end of the Civil War on the 4th of April 1865. However, the war wasn't officially completed until the 20th of August in 1866.

ANDREW JOHNSON

That was the date when President Andrew Johnson, who was President after Lincoln, placed his signature on a document stating that the United States of America was at peace and the war was over.

PRESIDENT LINCOLN IS KILLED

The well-known, wealthy actor, John Wilkes Booth, who hated Lincoln and the abolitionists, assassinated him by shooting him in the back of the head. Lincoln and his wife were watching a performance at Ford's Theater when Booth assassinated him on the 14th of April in 1865.

Ga. R. R. 1675

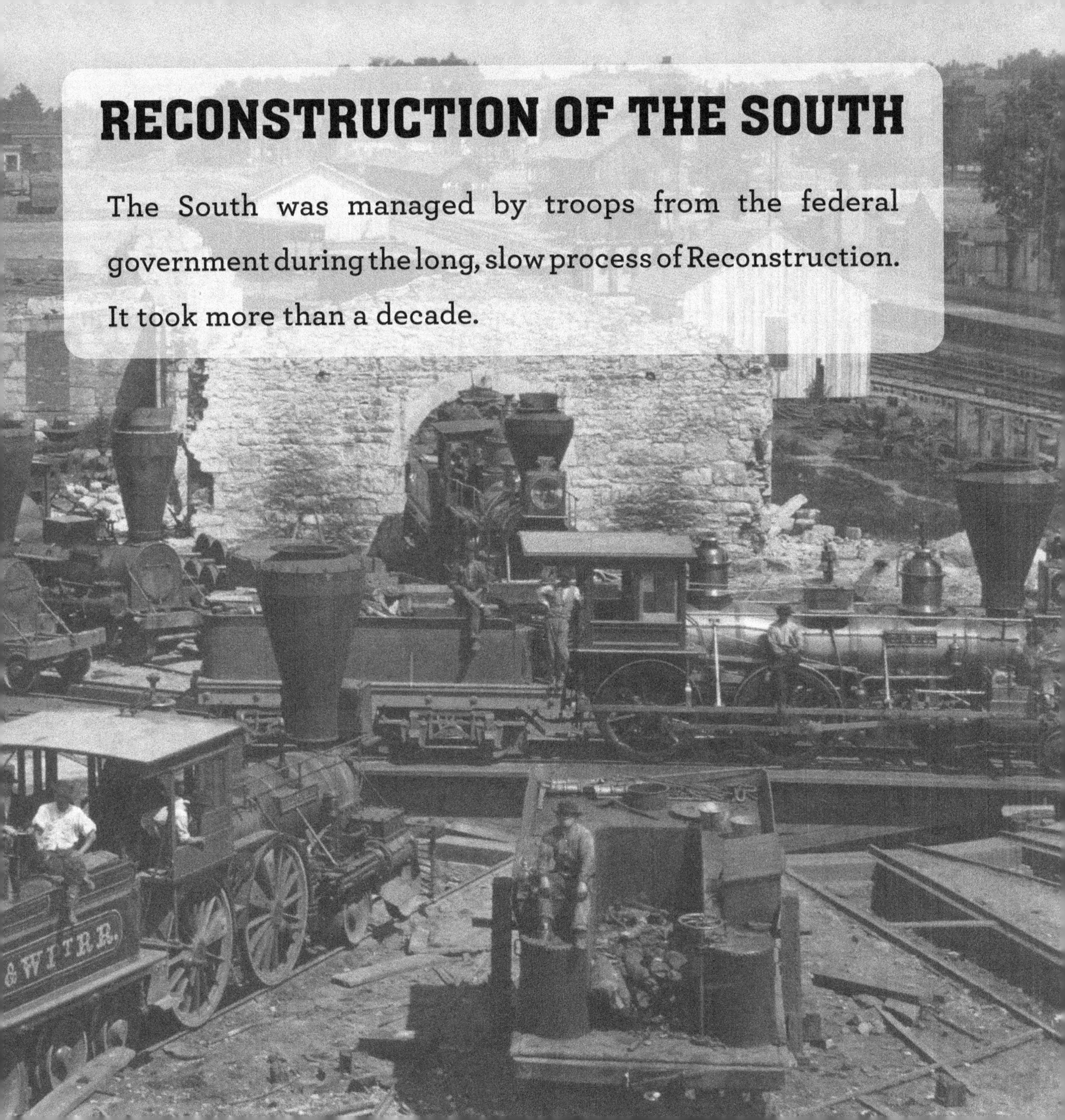

RECONSTRUCTION OF THE SOUTH

The South was managed by troops from the federal government during the long, slow process of Reconstruction. It took more than a decade.

&WITRR.

SUMMARY

The unrest between the southern states and northern states of the US began in 1860 and didn't come to a close until 1865. The southern states seceded to form the Confederate States of America.

They lost the Civil War and were brought back into the United States. There were many reasons that the southern states were unhappy and didn't want to remain in the United States, but the major reason was they didn't want slavery abolished. Over 600,000 soldiers died during the Civil War.

Now that you've read about the American Civil War, you may want to read more about women who were former slaves and then fought for freedom in the Baby Professor book From Slaves to Liberators: Stories of Women Who Fought for Freedom – Biography 5th Grade.

Visit

BABY PROFESSOR
EDUCATION KIDS

www.BabyProfessorBooks.com

to download Free Baby Professor eBooks
and view our catalog of new and exciting
Children's Books